FOR ORGANS, PIANOS & ELECTRONIC KEYBOARDS

179

LOVE SON
BEA

M000159507

ISBN 978-0-7935-3365-7

HAL•LEONARD®
CORPORATION
7777 W. BLUEMOUND RD. P.O. BOX 13819 MILWAUKEE, WI 53213

All My Loving

Registration 9
Rhythm: Rock

Words and Music by John Lennon
and Paul McCartney

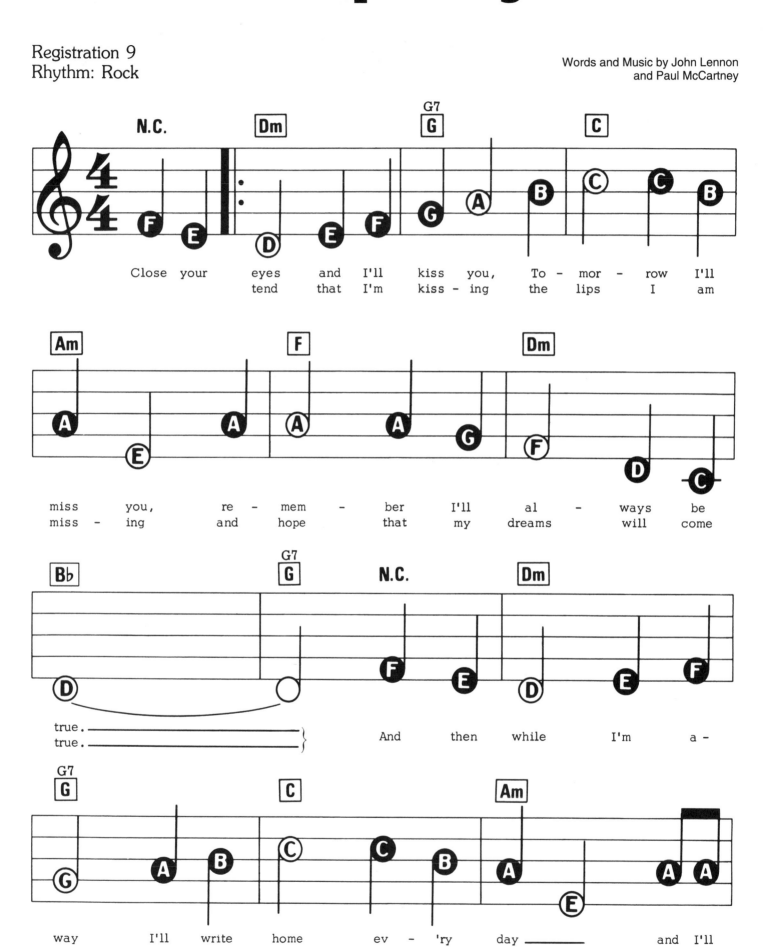

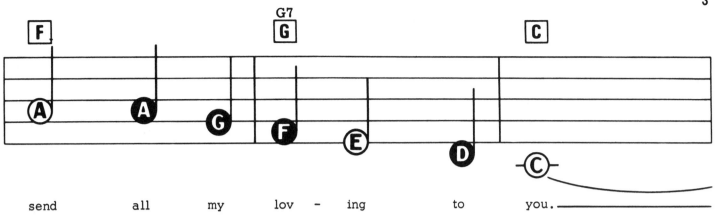

send   all   my   lov – ing   to   you. _____

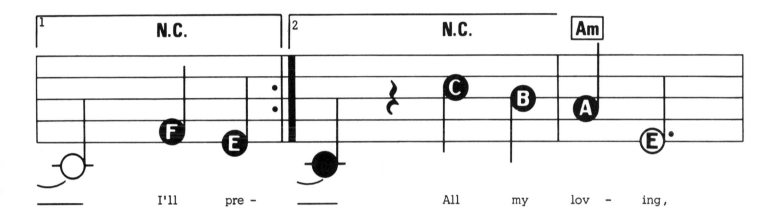

_____   I'll   pre – _____   All   my   lov – ing,

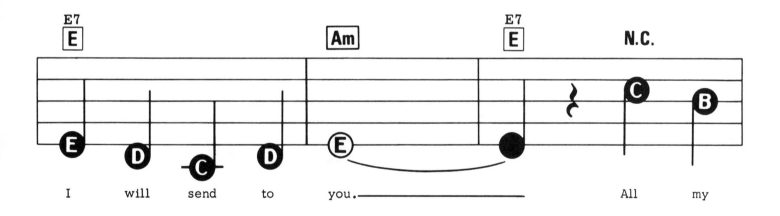

I   will   send   to   you. _____   All   my

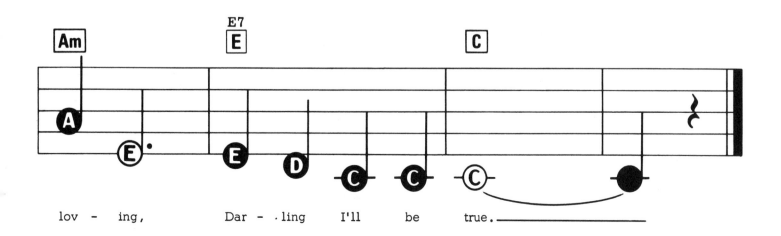

lov – ing,   Dar – ling   I'll   be   true. _____

And I Love Her

Registration 8
Rhythm: Rock or Jazz Rock

Words and Music by John Lennon
and Paul McCartney

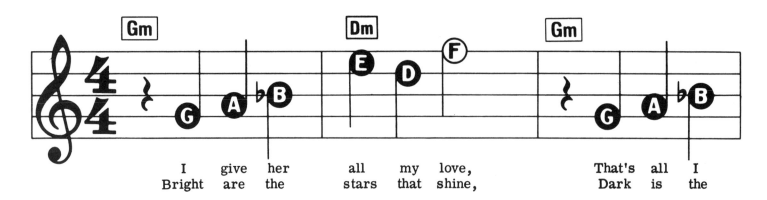

I give her all my love,   That's all I
Bright are the stars that shine,   Dark is the

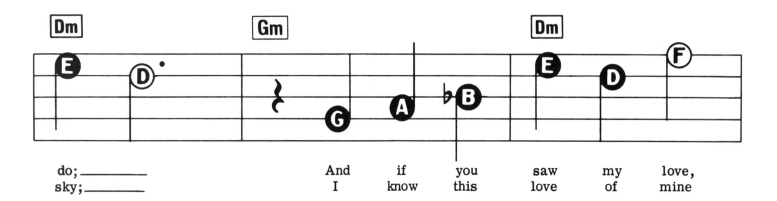

do; _____   And if you saw my love,
sky; _____   I know this love of mine

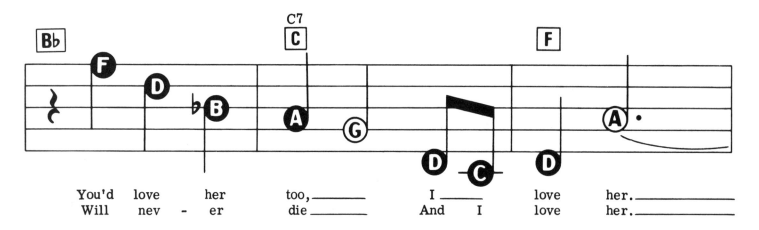

You'd love her too, _____   I _____ love her. _____
Will nev - er die _____   And I love her. _____

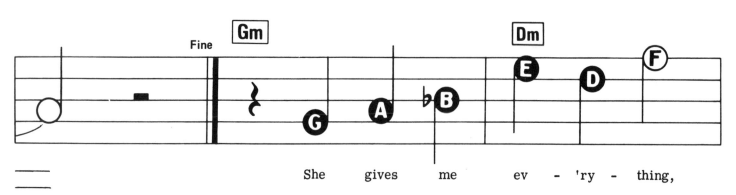

She gives me ev - 'ry - thing,

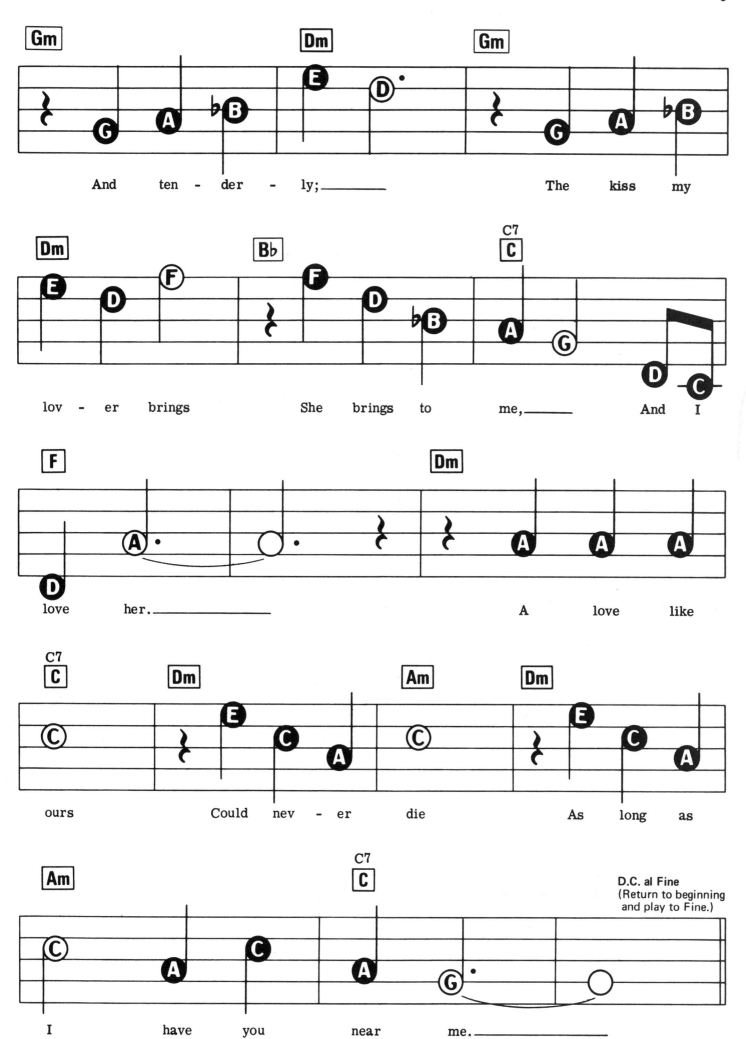

All You Need Is Love

Registration 5
Rhythm: Shuffle or Swing

Words and Music by John Lennon
and Paul McCartney

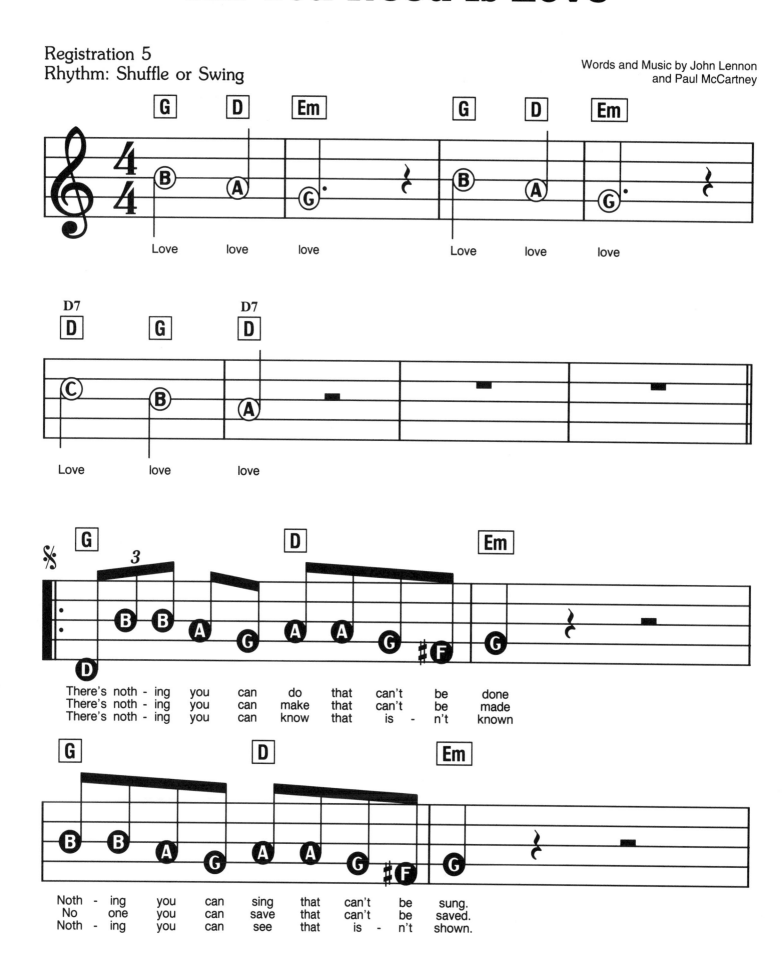

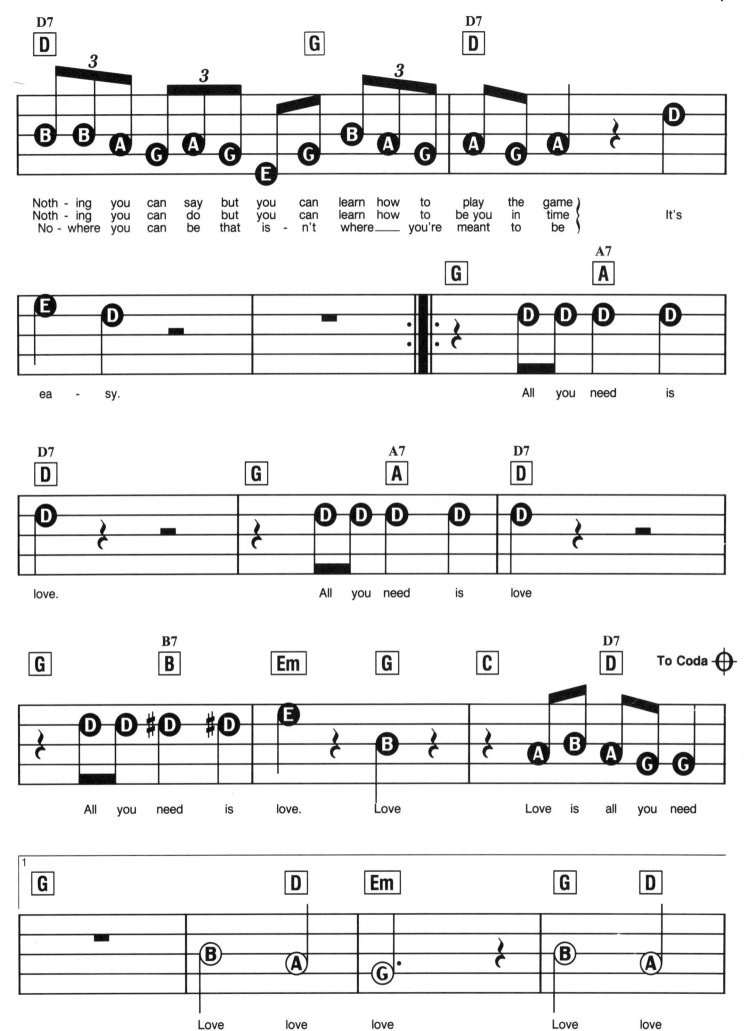

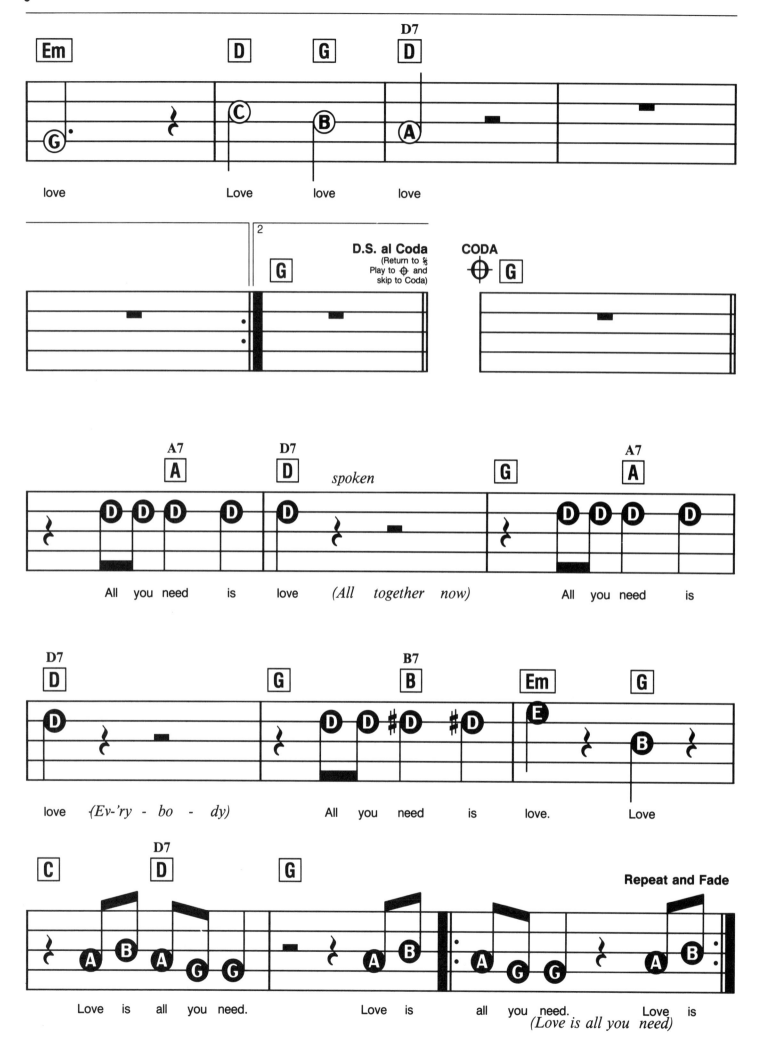

Girl

Registration 2
Rhythm: Shuffle or Swing

Words and Music by
John Lennon and Paul McCartney

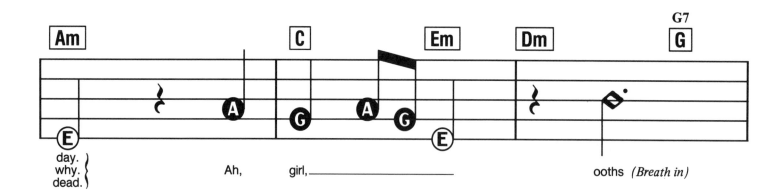

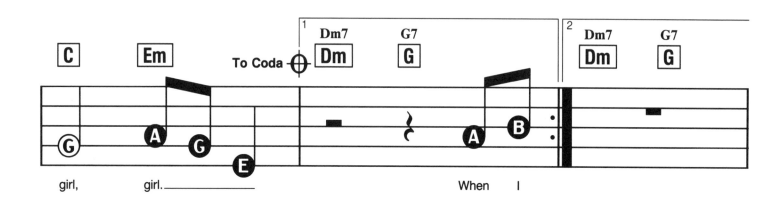

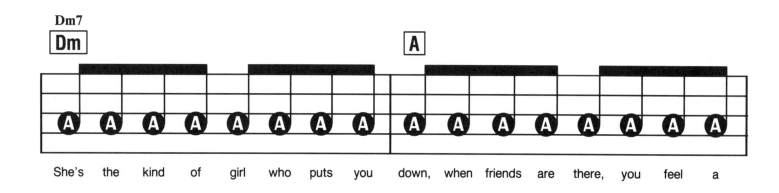

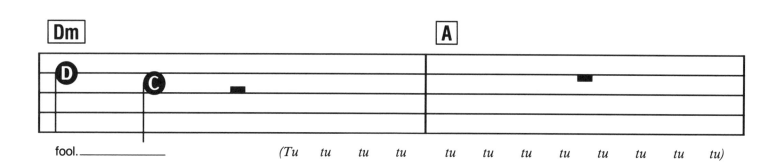

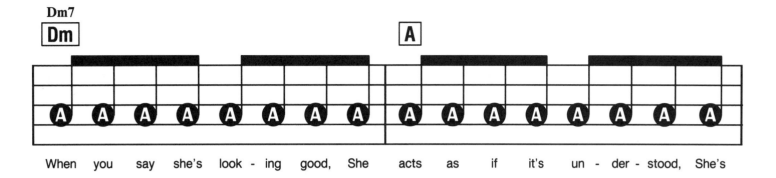

When you say she's look - ing good, She acts as if it's un - der - stood, She's

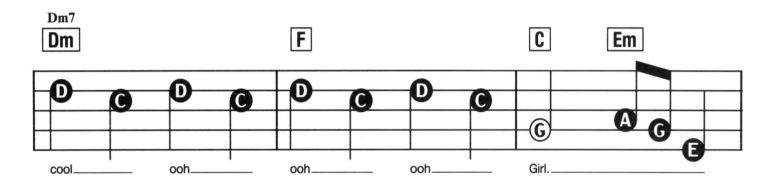

cool_____ ooh ooh ooh Girl._____

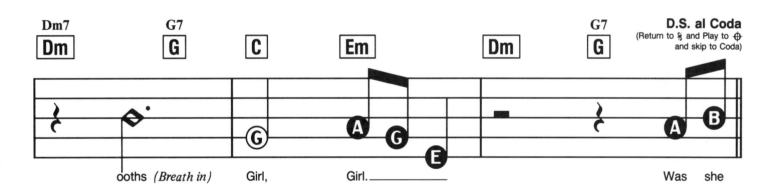

ooths *(Breath in)* Girl, Girl._____ Was she

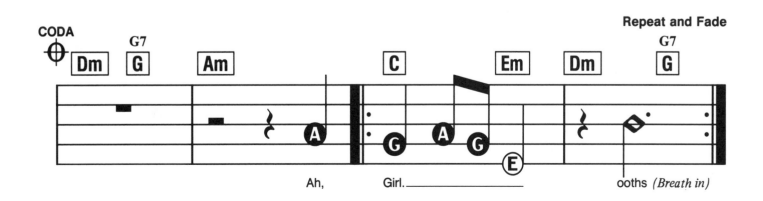

Ah, Girl._____ ooths *(Breath in)*

Eight Days A Week

Registration 2
Rhythm: Rock

Words and Music by John Lennon
and Paul McCartney

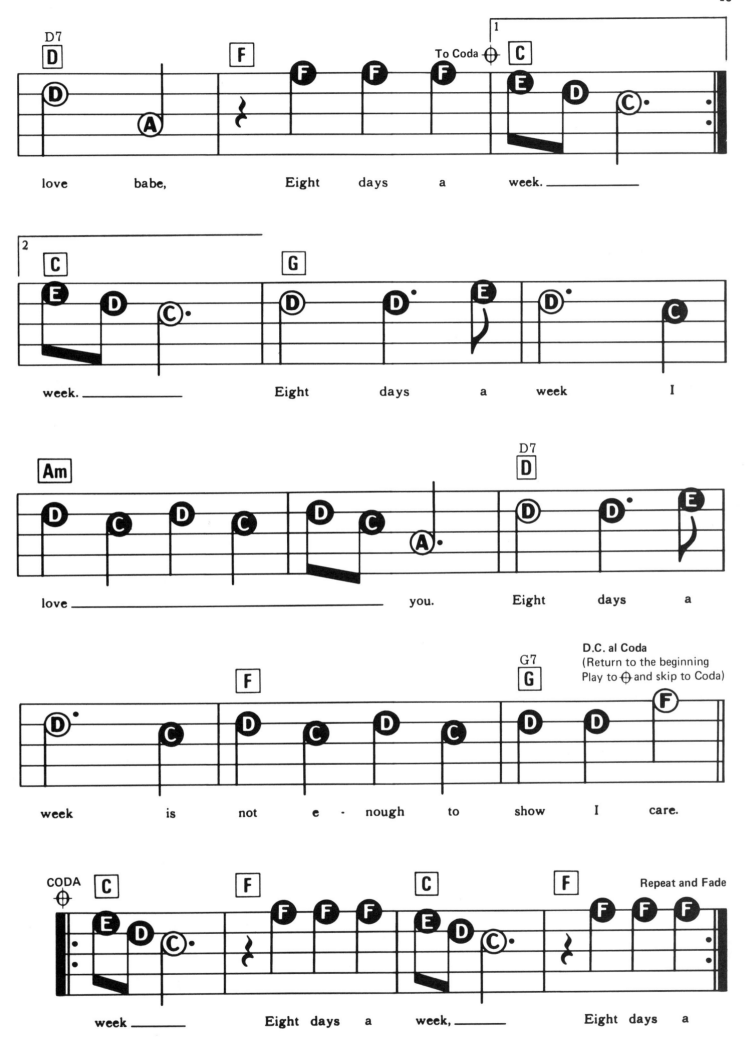

From Me To You

Registration 7
Rhythm: Rock

Words and Music by
John Lennon and Paul McCartney

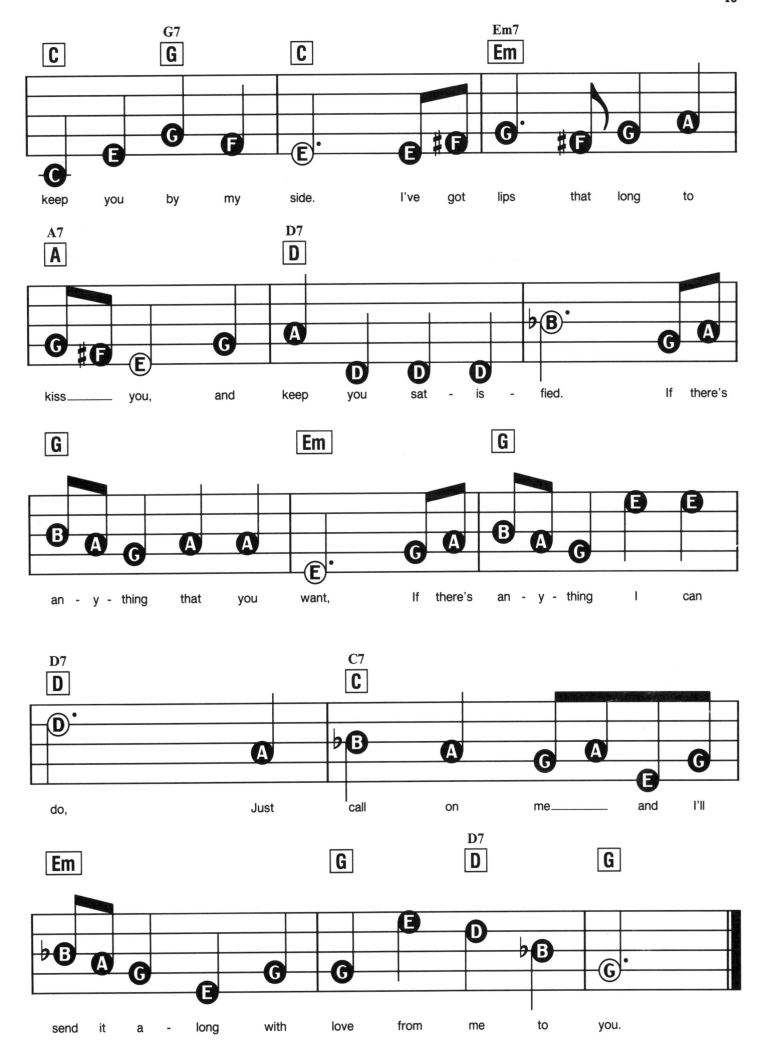

Here, There And Everywhere

Registration 2
Rhythm: Rock or Jazz Rock

Words and Music by
John Lennon and Paul McCartney

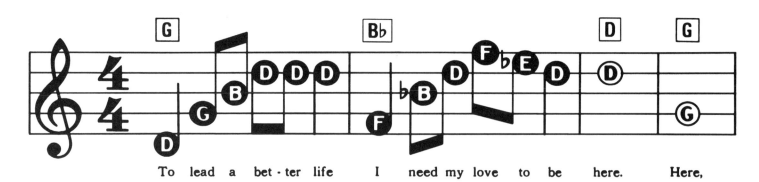

To lead a bet-ter life I need my love to be here. Here,

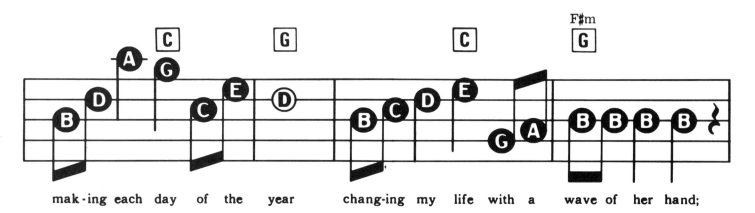

mak-ing each day of the year chang-ing my life with a wave of her hand;

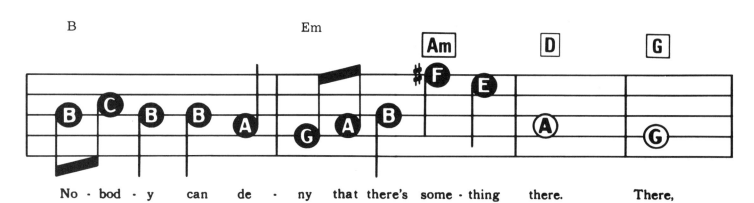

No-bod-y can de-ny that there's some-thing there. There,

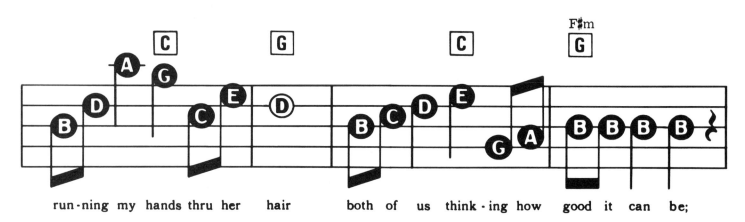

run-ning my hands thru her hair both of us think-ing how good it can be;

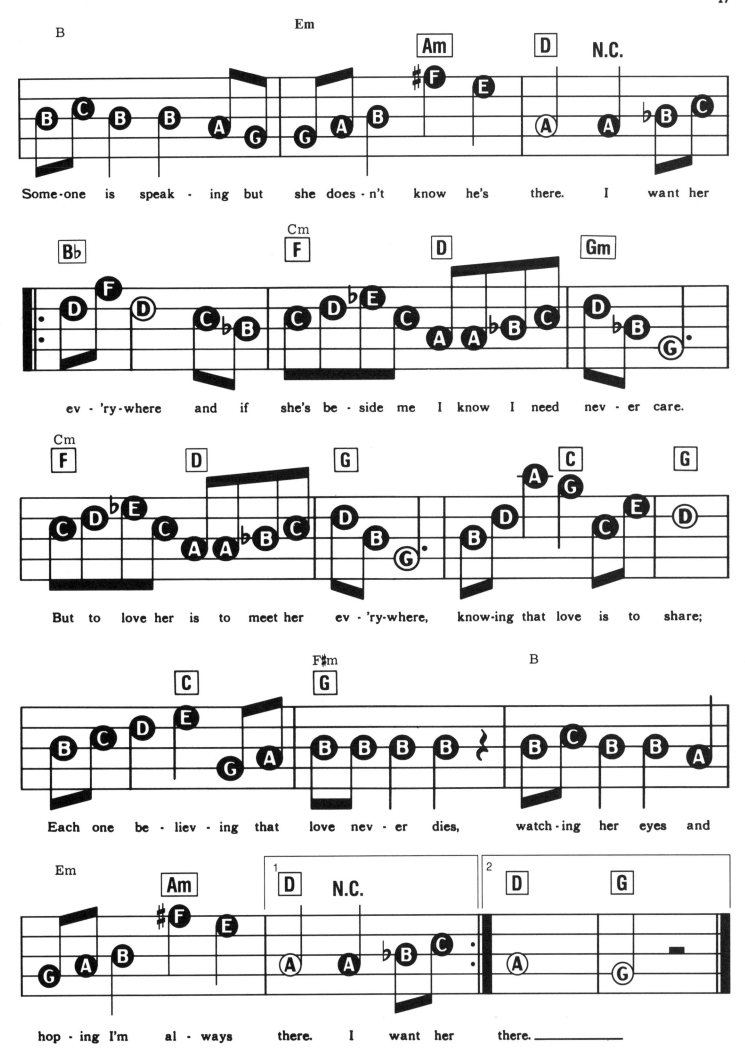

Hey Jude

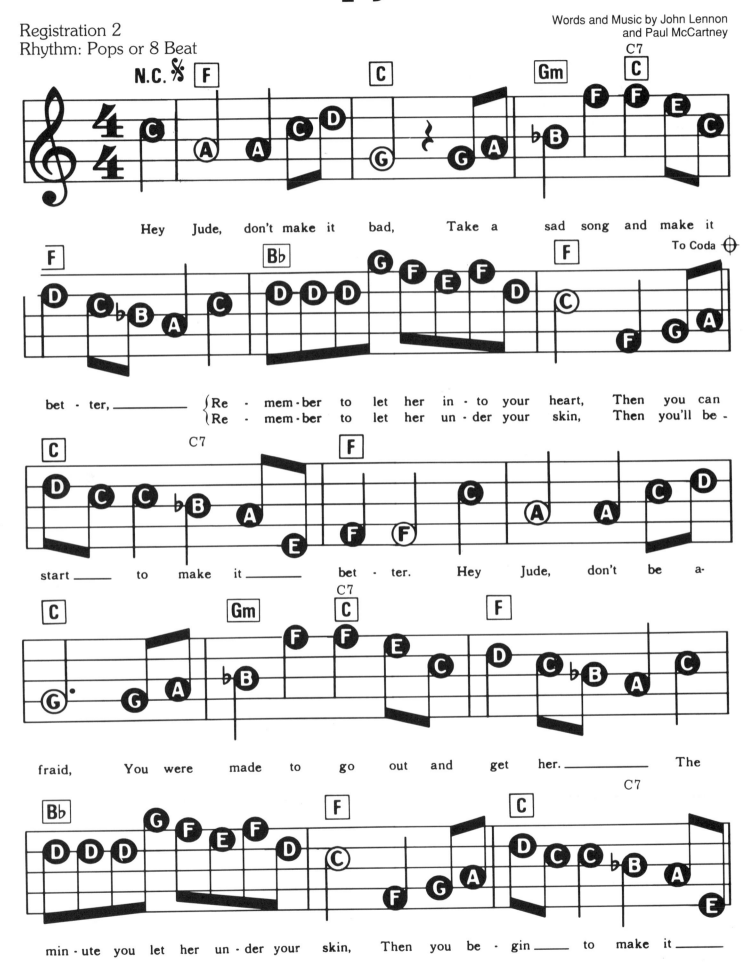

Registration 2
Rhythm: Pops or 8 Beat

Words and Music by John Lennon
and Paul McCartney

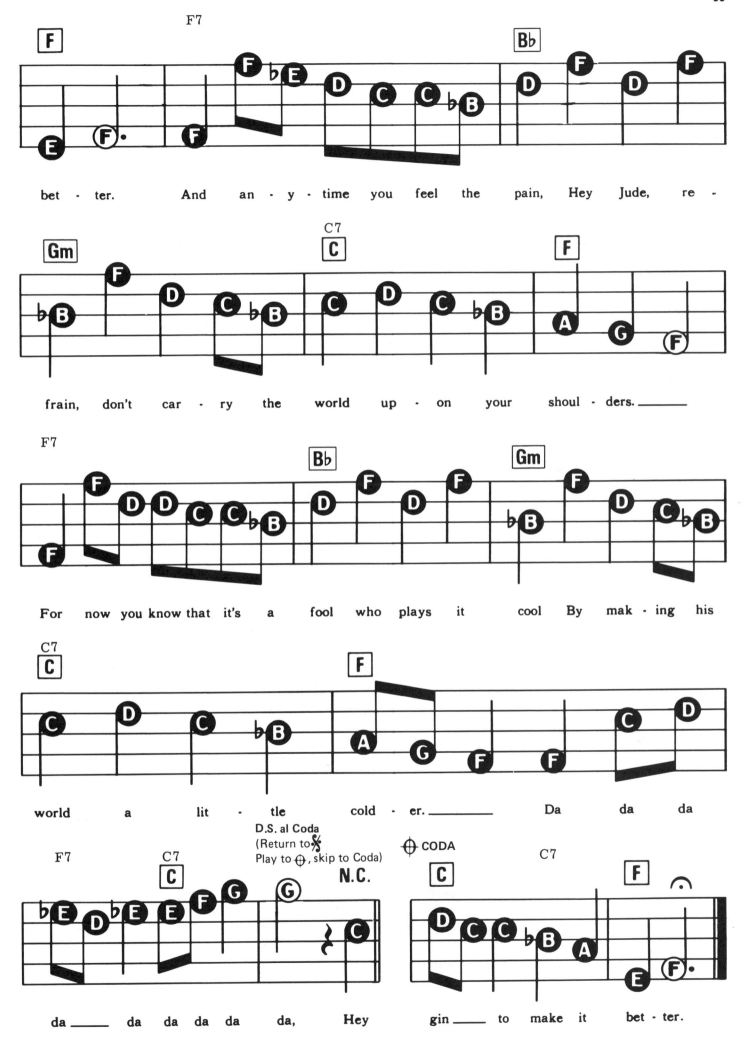

I Will

Registration 4
Rhythm: Rock or Slow Rock

Words and Music by
John Lennon and Paul McCartney

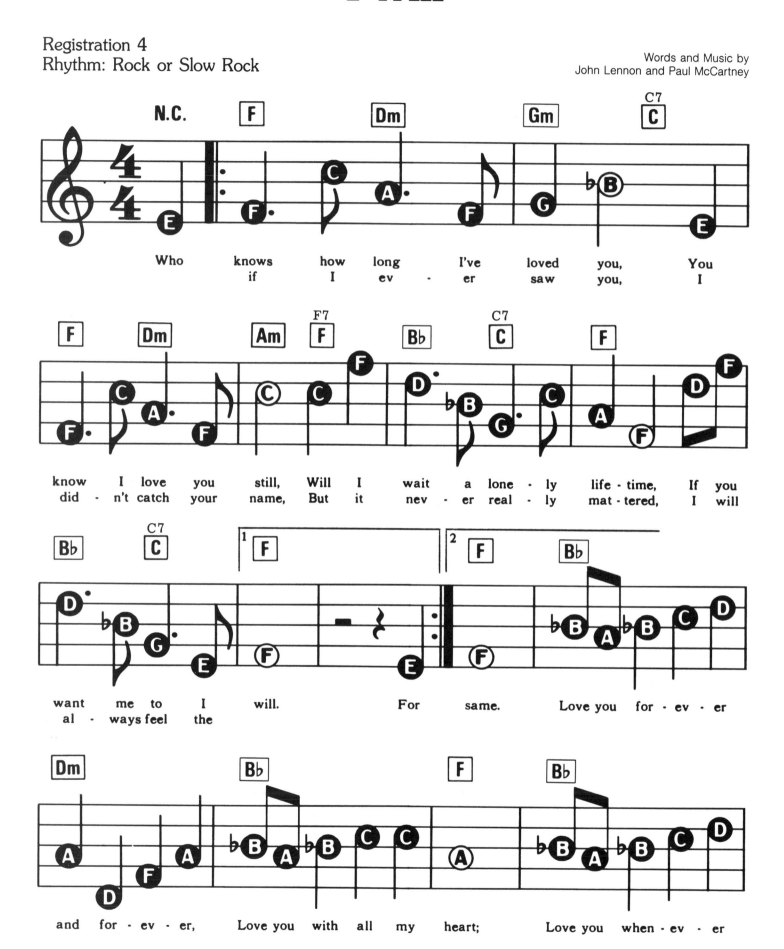

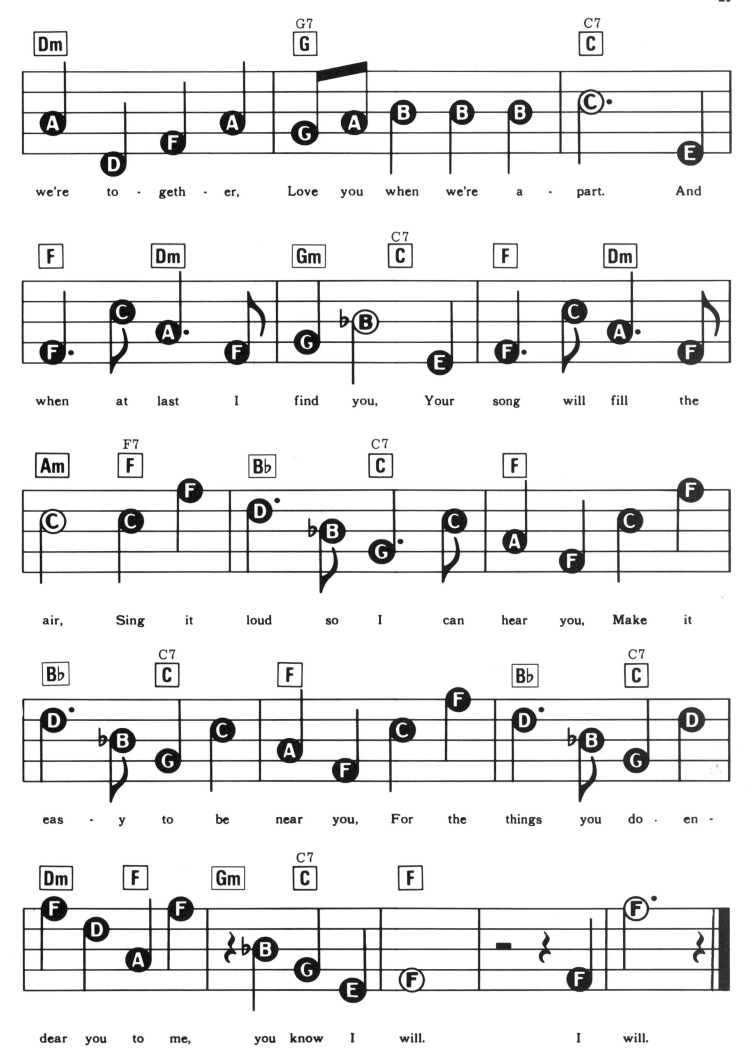

If I Fell

Registration 9
Rhythm: Rock or Latin

Words and Music by
John Lennon and Paul McCartney

If I give my heart to you I
trust my in you to oh you please I don't

must be sure from the ve - ry start that you would
run and sure hide if I love you too oh you please don't

love me more than her
hurt my pride like her 'Cos I

could - n't stand the pain And I would be sad if our new

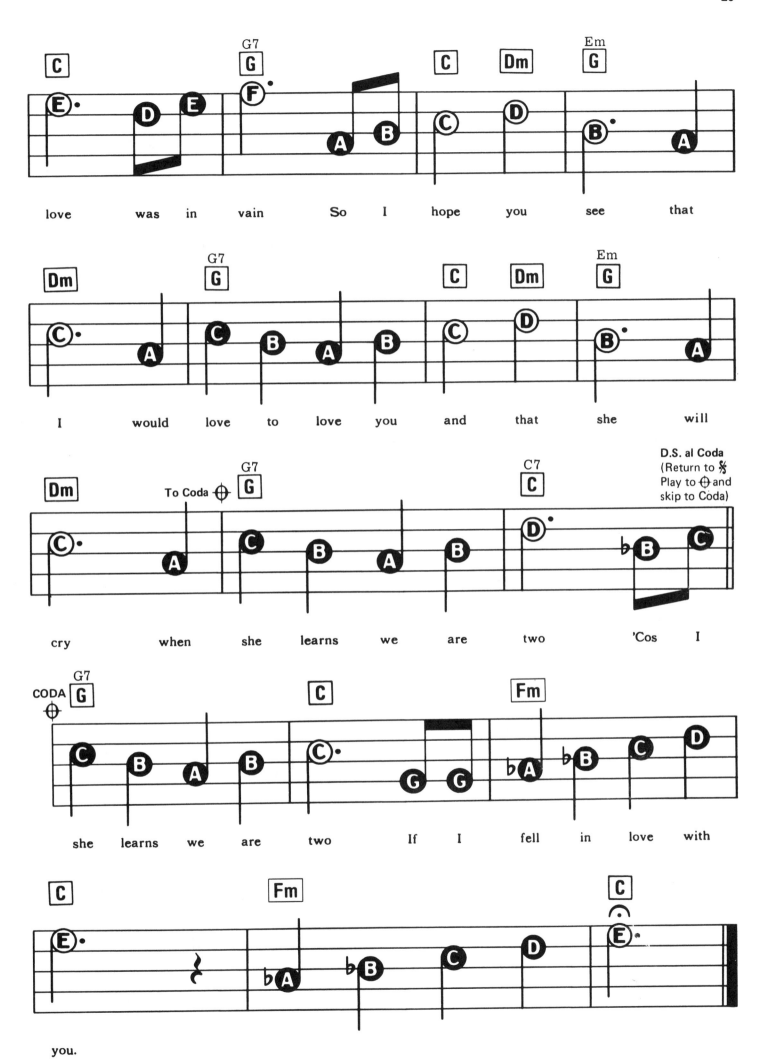

In My Life

Registration 3
Rhythm: Rock

Words and Music by
John Lennon and Paul McCartney

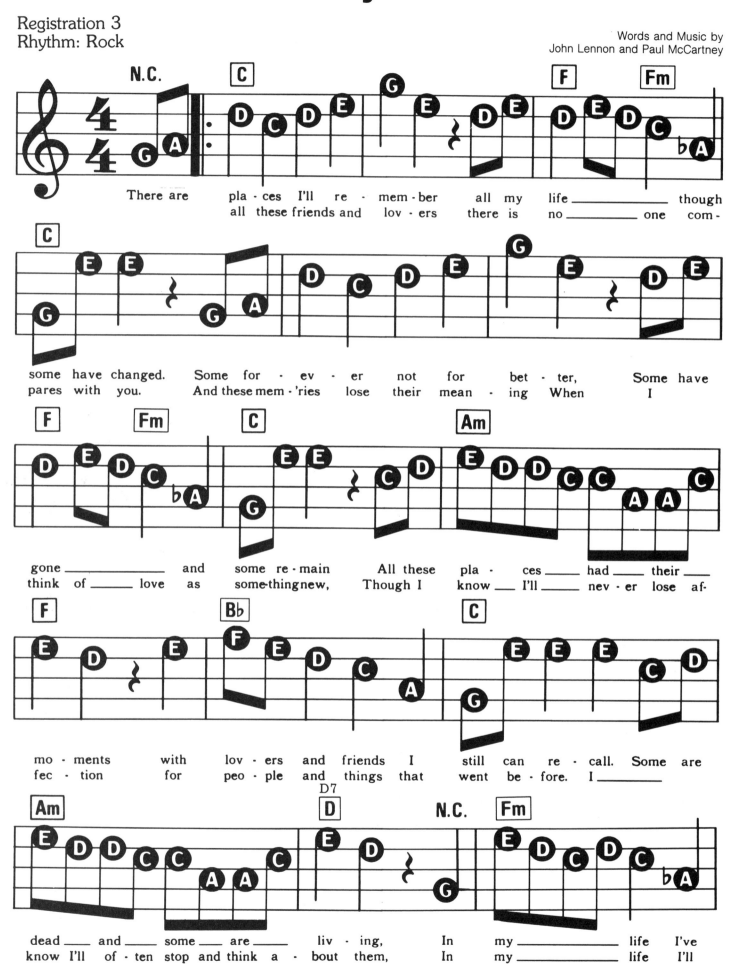

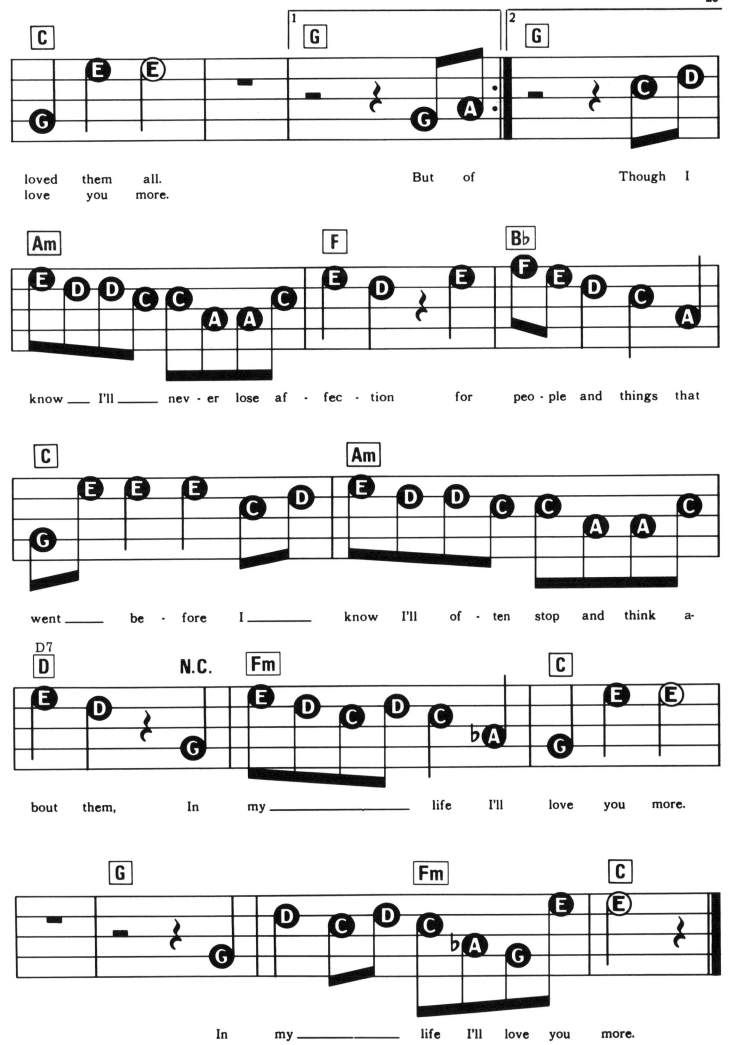

It's Only Love

Registration 4
Rhythm: Rock

Words and Music by
John Lennon and Paul McCartney

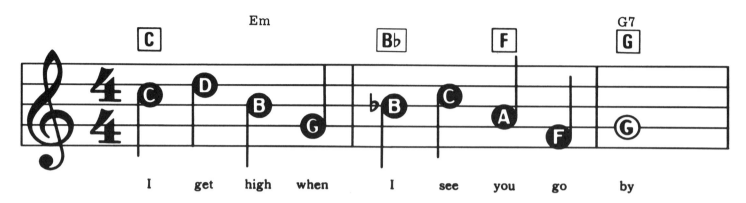

I get high when I see you go by

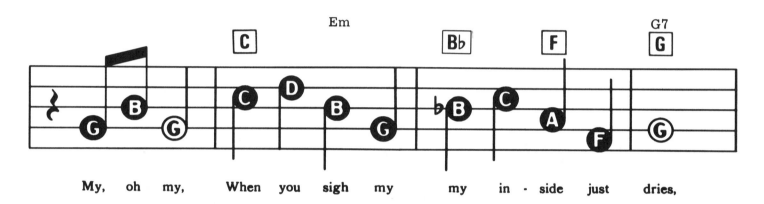

My, oh my, When you sigh my my in - side just dries,

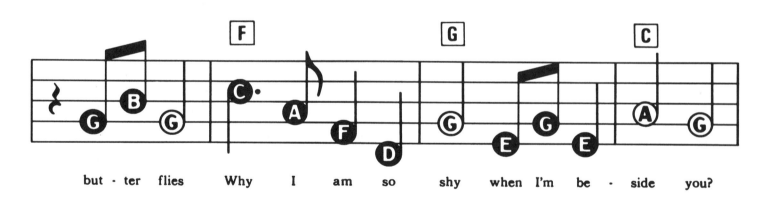

but - ter flies Why I am so shy when I'm be - side you?

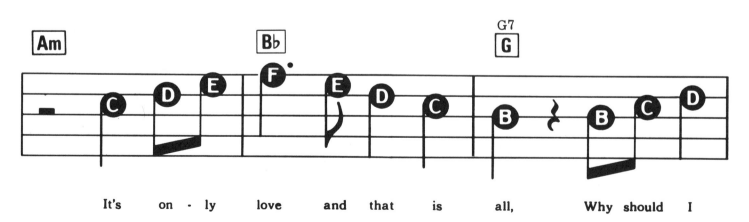

It's on - ly love and that is all, Why should I

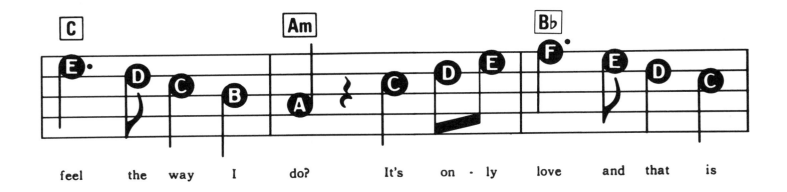

feel the way I do? It's on-ly love and that is

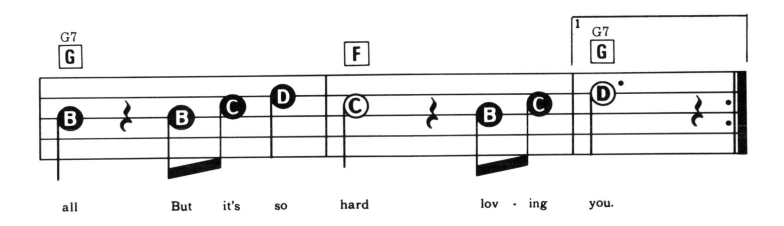

all But it's so hard lov - ing you.

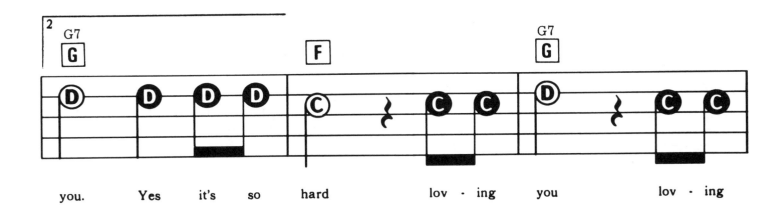

you. Yes it's so hard lov - ing you lov - ing

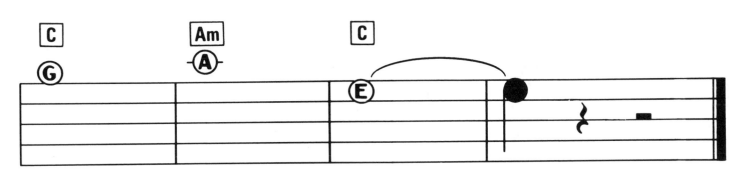

you. _____

I'm Happy Just To Dance With You

Registration 4
Rhythm: Rock

Words and Music by
John Lennon and Paul McCartney

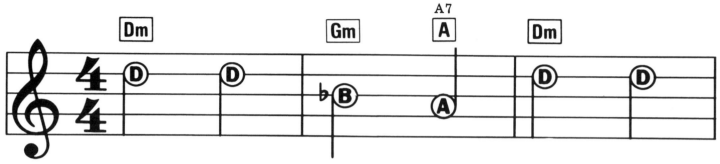

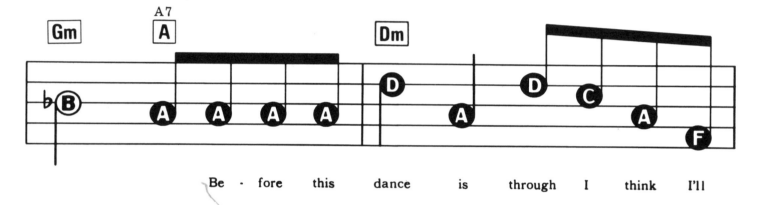

Be - fore this dance is through I think I'll

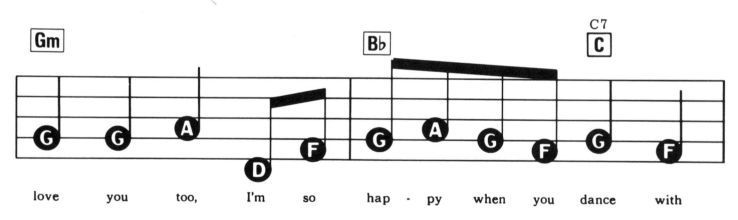

love you too, I'm so hap - py when you dance with

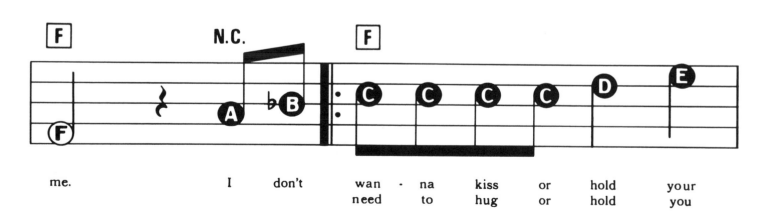

me.   I don't   wan - na   kiss   or   hold   your

             need   to   hug   or   hold   you

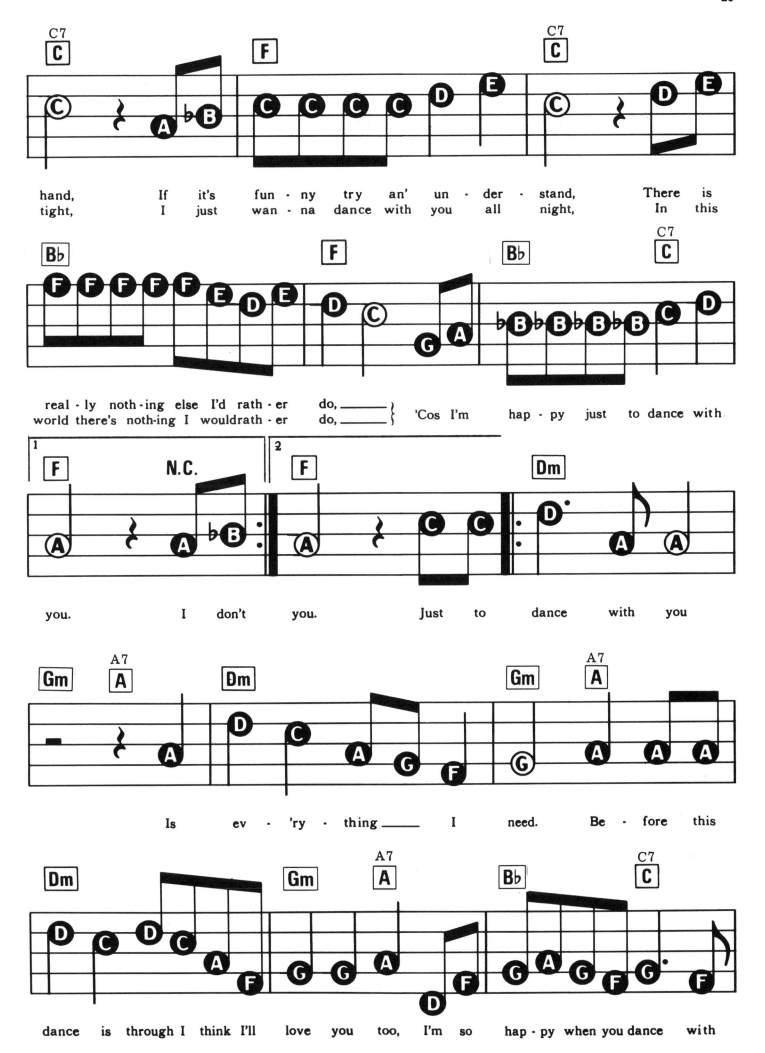

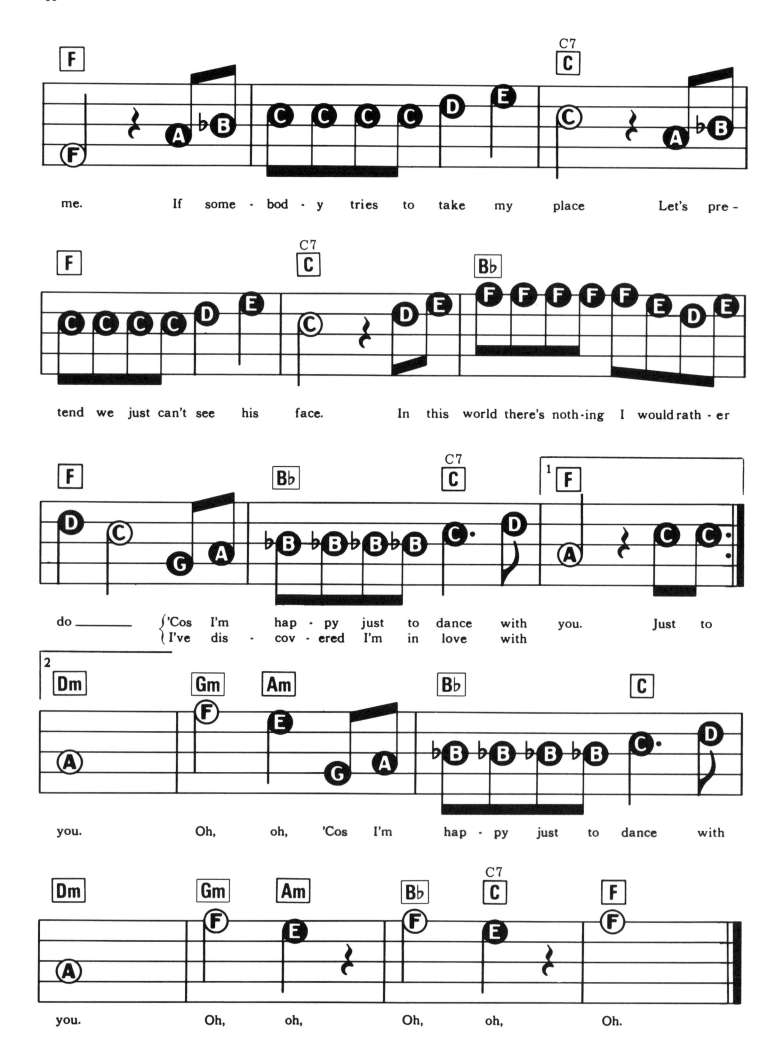

The Long And Winding Road

Registration 4
Rhythm: Rock and Slow Rock

Words and Music by John Lennon
and Paul McCartney

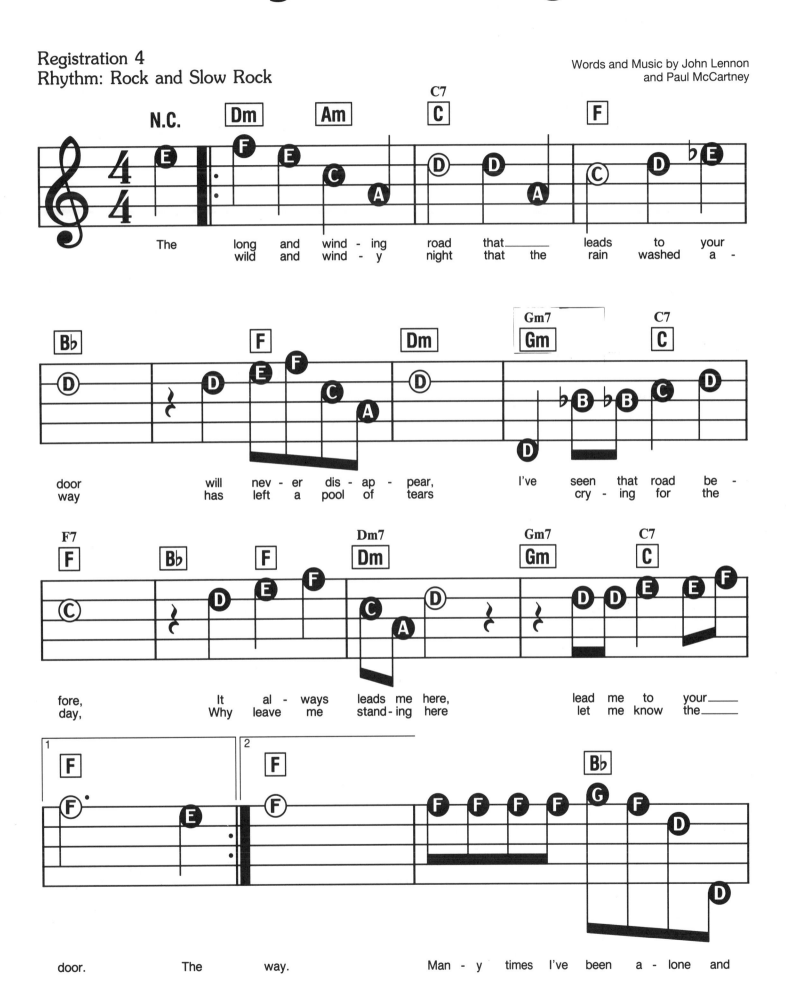

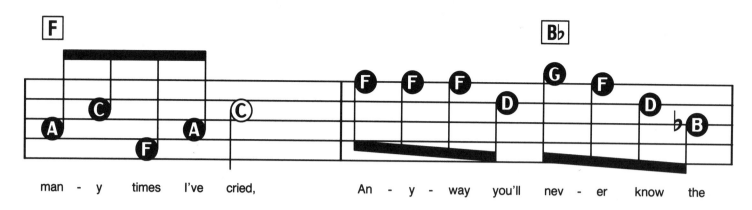

man - y times I've cried, An - y - way you'll nev - er know the

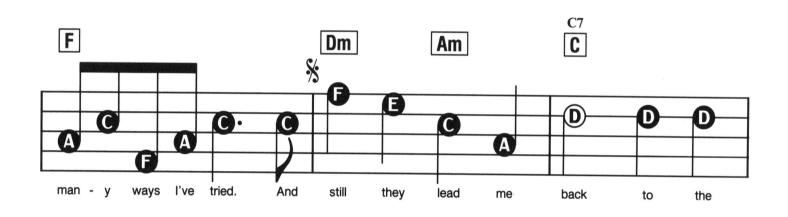

man - y ways I've tried. And still they lead me back to the

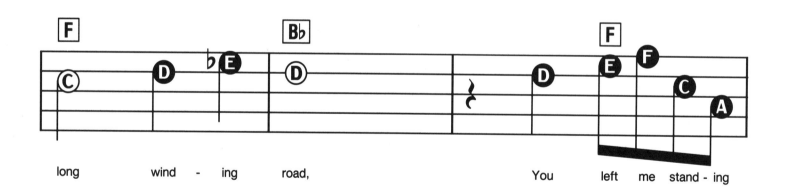

long wind - ing road, You left me stand - ing

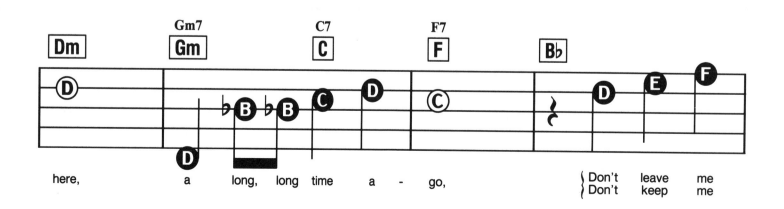

here, a long, long time a - go, Don't leave me / Don't keep me

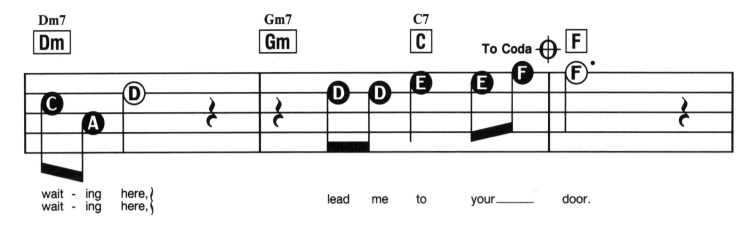

wait - ing here,
wait - ing here,

lead me to your____ door.

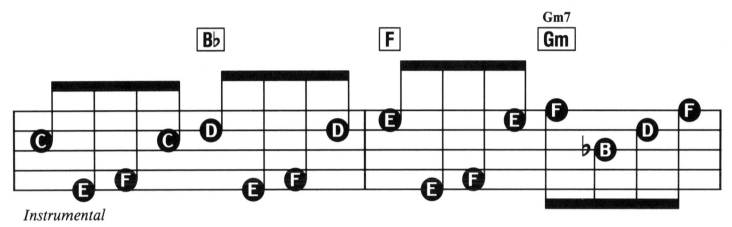

Instrumental

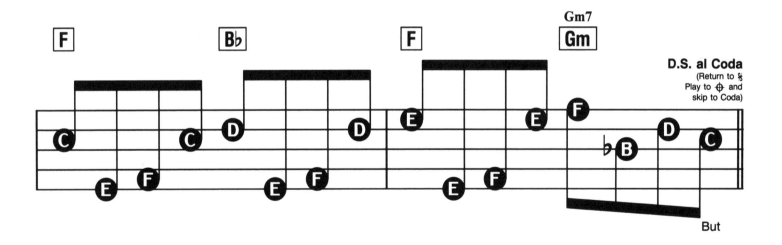

But

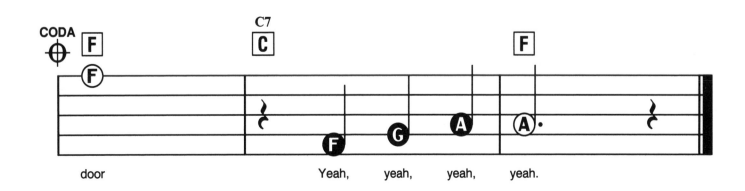

door

Yeah, yeah, yeah, yeah.

Julia

Registration 4
Rhythm: Rock

Words and Music by
John Lennon and Paul McCartney

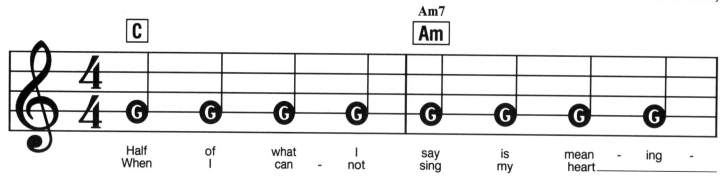

Half   of   what   I   say   is   mean - ing -
When   I   can - not   sing   my   heart_____

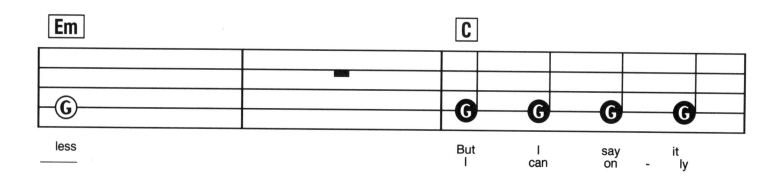

less   But   I   say   it
_____   I   can   on - ly

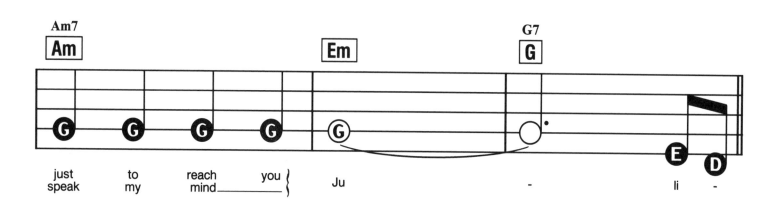

just   to   reach   you {   Ju
speak   my   mind_____

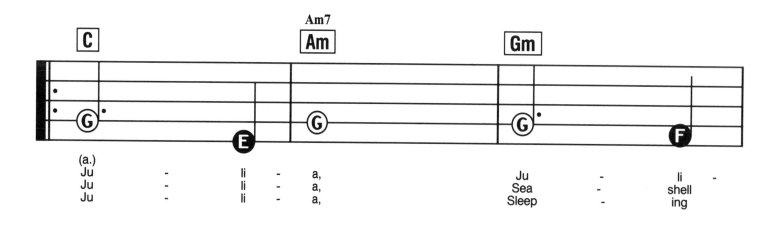

(a.)
Ju - li - a,   Ju - li -
Ju - li - a,   Sea - shell
Ju - li - a,   Sleep - ing

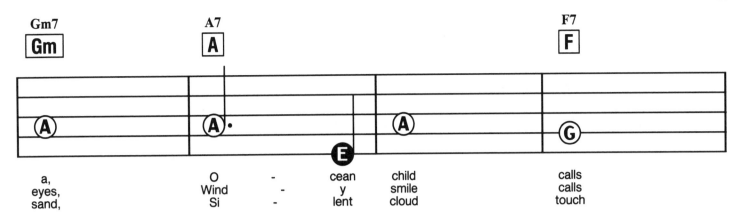

a,
eyes,
sand,

O - cean child   calls
Wind - y smile   calls
Si - lent cloud   touch

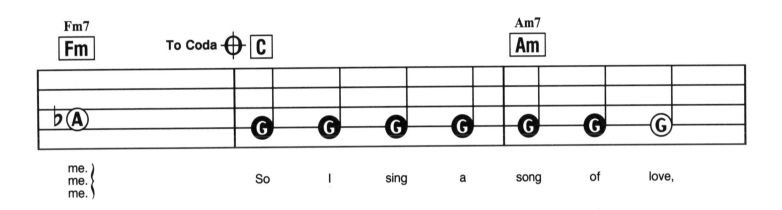

me.
me.
me.

So I sing a song of love,

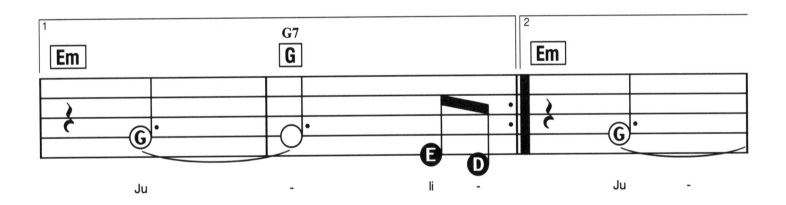

Ju - li -   Ju -

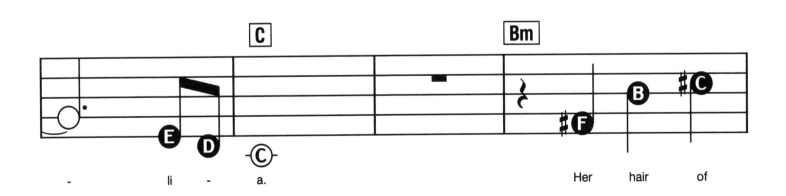

- li - a.   Her hair of

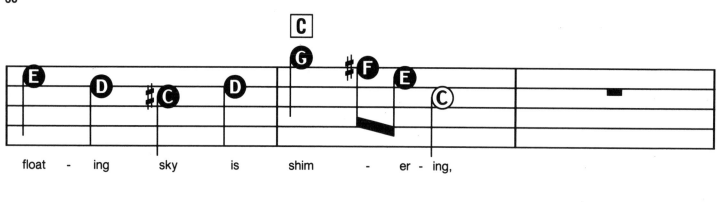

float - ing sky is shim - er - ing,

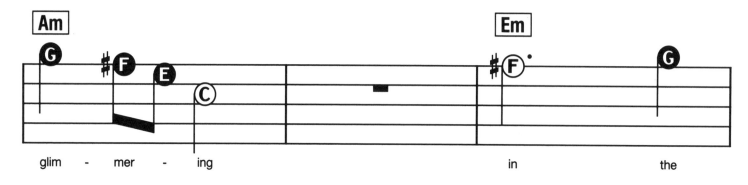

glim - mer - ing   in   the

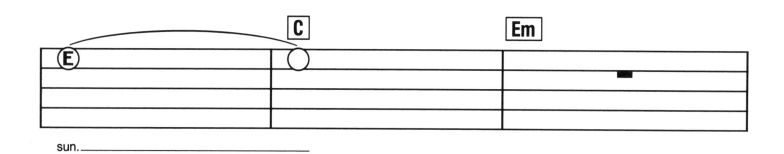

sun.

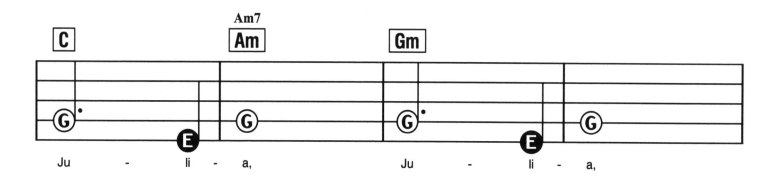

Ju - li - a,   Ju - li - a,

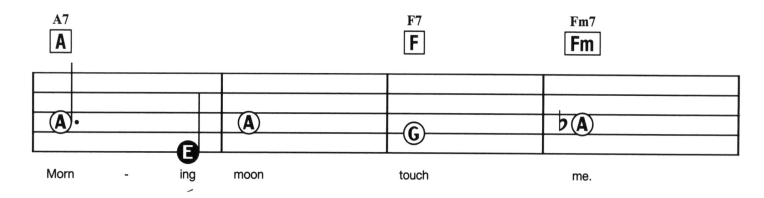

Morn - ing moon   touch   me.

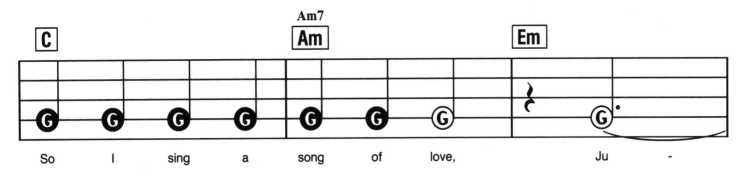

So I sing a song of love, Ju -

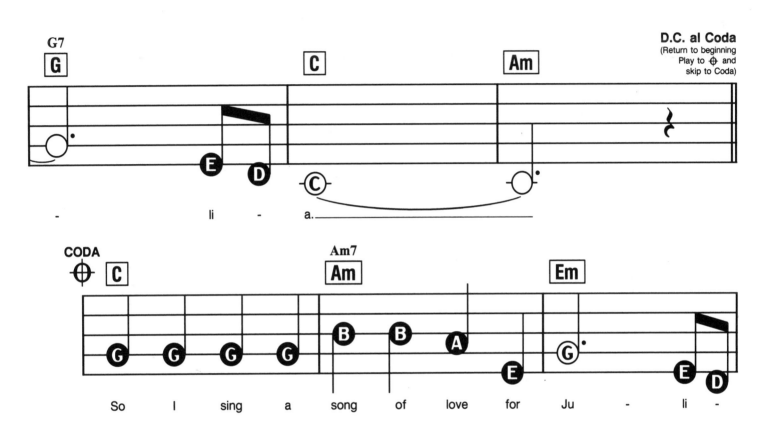

D.C. al Coda
(Return to beginning
Play to ⊕ and
skip to Coda)

- li - a. _____

CODA

So I sing a song of love for Ju - li -

a, Ju - li - a,

Ju - li - a.

Michelle

Registration 1
Rhythm: Rock

Words and Music by John Lennon
and Paul McCartney

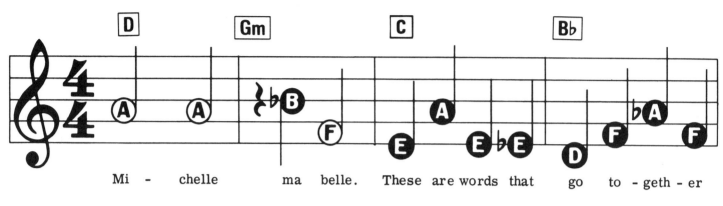

Mi - chelle ma belle. These are words that go to - geth - er

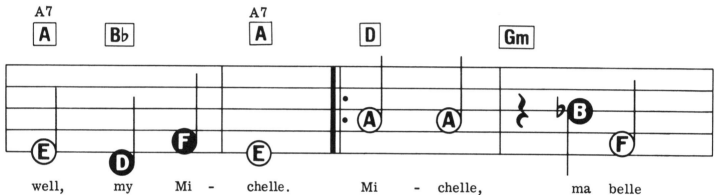

well, my Mi - chelle. Mi - chelle, ma belle

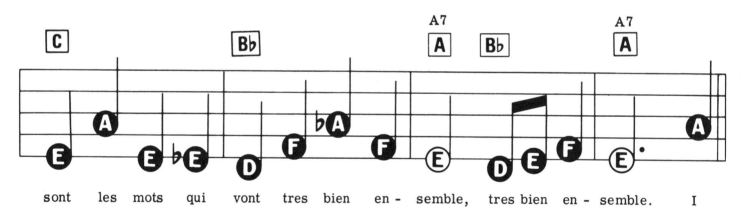

sont les mots qui vont tres bien en - semble, tres bien en - semble. I

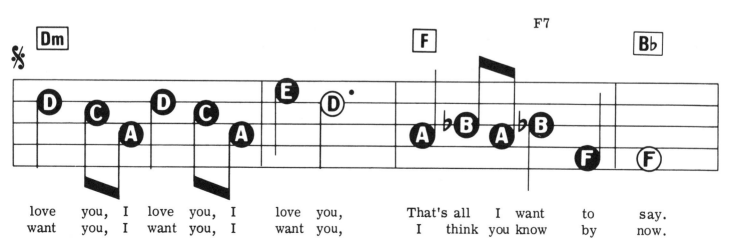

love you, I love you, I love you, That's all I want to say.
want you, I want you, I want you, I think you know by now.

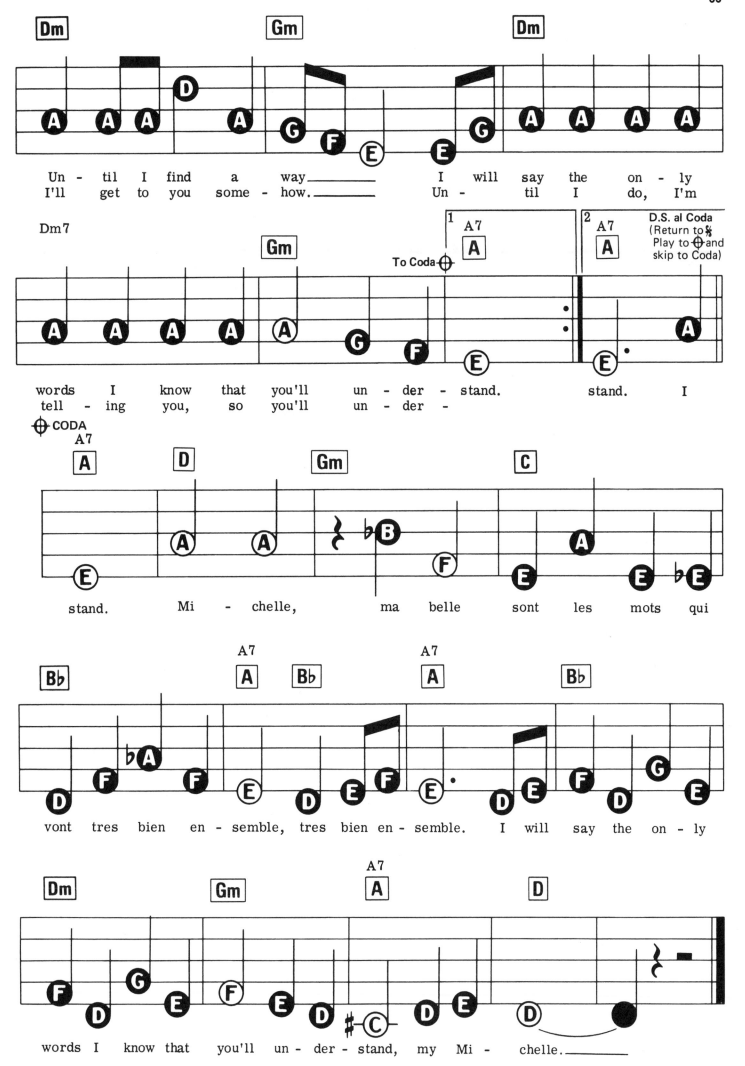

Something

Registration 4
Rhythm: Rock

By George Harrison

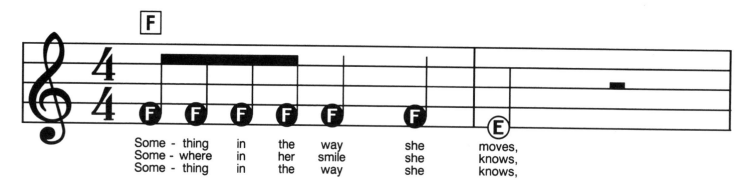

Some - thing in the way she moves,
Some - where in her smile she knows,
Some - thing in the way she knows,

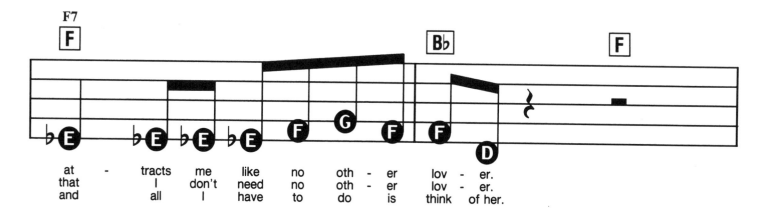

at - tracts me like no oth - er lov - er.
that I don't need no oth - er lov - er.
and all I have to do is think of her.

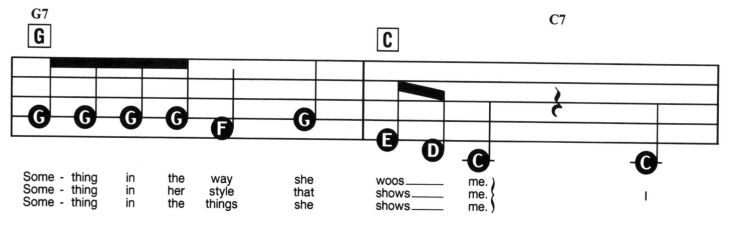

Some - thing in the way she woos____ me.
Some - thing in her style that shows____ me.
Some - thing in the things she shows____ me.

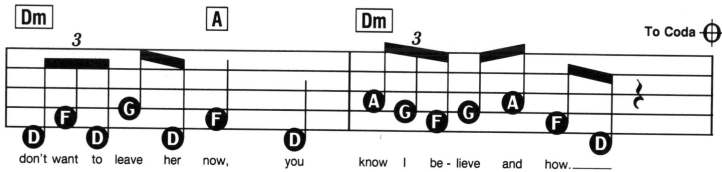

don't want to leave her now, you know I be - lieve and how.____

To Coda ⊕

Thank You Girl

Registration 5
Rhythm: Rock

Words and Music by
John Lennon and Paul McCartney

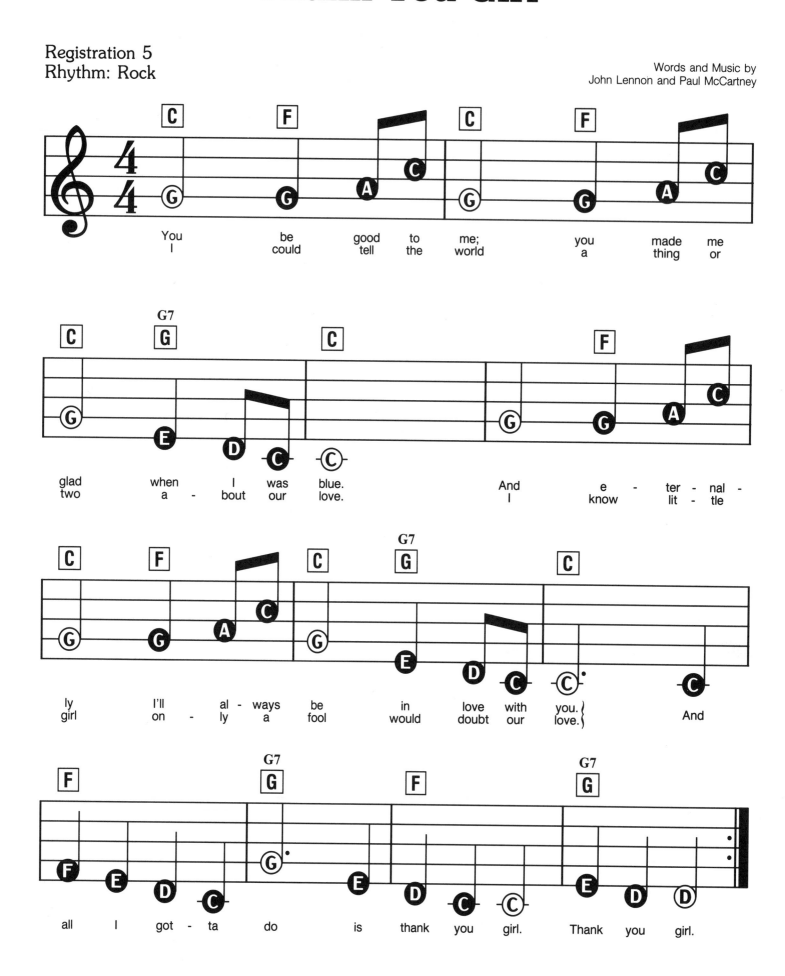